Italy
Valleys of Rock
Stephen Platt

www.leveretpublishing.com

Italy: Valleys of Rock
First published - August 2018
Published by
Leveret Publishing
56 Covent Garden, Cambridge, CB1 2HR, UK

Dimitri d'Andrea

ISBN 978-1-912460-22-9

© Stephen Platt 2018

All rights reserved. No part of this publication may be reproduced, stored in a retrieval system or transmitted in any form by any means, electronic, mechanical, photocopying, recording or otherwise, except brief extracts for the purpose of review, without the written permission of the publisher.

Italy
Valleys of Rock

Italy 2005

Florence

Friday 15 July

We had a good flight to Pisa and coach ride into Florence. This time Scharlie has not been consciously nervous of the trip and flying but all sorts of other symptoms have been plaguing her – a sore throat, stiffness in the lower back and pain all down her left leg and sciatic nerve, aching wrists and elbow joints, bloated stomach – she feels a total wreck!

We had only been at the bus stop a moment when Dimitri arrived with a fulsome welcome and drove us to his home in Sesto Firenze, Florence. He still hasn't finished his book, but he's putting it out of his head for this ten-day holiday, Teresa says. I tell him he must finish, but he says I just need to change this little bit. Walter and Mauri, who will be climbing with us, arrived about an hour after us and we shared a meal of pasta, wine from friends, cheese, and cake from Mauri's sister.

The conversation at supper is lively as usual – ranging from terrorism and global politics to personal relations and jealousy. Over pasta we talked the 'right man', a philosophical idea Dimitri was writing about. It is impossible to be jealous of Dimitri, says Teresa, he is completely monogamous! They see us as being a perfectly suited couple and Stephen the epitome of cheerfulness, kindness and reason! Haha.

Dimitri has so many guidebooks but he is still afraid to leave one he might need. The acolytes are reading the sacred texts, quips Steve. Scharlie's chief concern is to have the choice to stay in the campsite if she wants to and to be able to climb without a sack. Both these possibilities may be impossible though, if it inconveniences the rest of the party.

It is hot during the day, 32°, and we were restless in the night until we put the conditioning on. The blackout blinds means we sleep till 8:45 AM, despite painfully descending the hit and miss stairs to the loo three times in the night. It is very hot and sticky today and the air conditioning just makes it feel normal! Scharlie has already lost her glasses case, so she is not doing too well – but Dimitri and Teresa are so nice to be with it doesn't matter.

Valle Maira

Saturday 16 July 2005

This morning, over breakfast, we continue the ritual of the guidebooks. He shows us a photo of where he plans to take us – Roca Castello in Valle Maira, near the French border in Provence. It looks harder this morning, than when you showed it us last night, says Steve. They laugh, but the article he had shown us last night made it look more benign and attractive than did these route photos in the guide this morning.

The books had come out the night before – pulled out of a canvas sack dedicated to guidebooks. Over the meal and wine the conversation had been animated and positive. Now the mood is more sombre.

We leave at 11.30 for a four-hour drive to via Genoa to Chiappera near the French border. It's in the Maritime Alps and is billed as the Dolomites transplanted. We didn't decide which part of Italy to go until late last night. Dimitri likes discussion – we have these possibilities, he says. However, we are not much use to him. Walter and Mauri aren't much better and Dimitri became exasperated for a few minutes, but then recovers his good humour. Dimitri knows Steve has a passion for cheese and we stop near Castell Magno to buy some of its famous cheese, a little like Parmesan. Cheese doesn't seem to travel well to England, so it's a great pleasure to nibble it here with dry biscuits impregnated with herbs.

We drove through Genoa and on through Dronero, where they are getting ready for a festival. At Caraglio, about 80 km south west of Turin, Teresa said they made the best cheese in the world just up the valley at Castel Magno. We past a shop advertising Formaggio e Latte, cheese and milk. I asked if one could buy the cheese there. Yes, said Dimitri and drove on. I looked at Scharlie and then he caught on and turned around and bought two types of cheese.

We continued up the valley to Chiappera. Dimitri said the area had been very depressed and run-down but had received EU funding over the last few years and was expanding. You could see the effect in the renovated houses in the village. After a walk we carried on to a refuge. We are camping at Campo Base in Teresa's tent. She bought it for a good price last year and we are christening it. It's a three-man tent, so luxury for us with our inflatable mattresses and pillows brought from Florence. They are sleeping in their car on a double mattress on top of a built in chest of drawers. Their car, a bright yellow Renault Kangoo, doesn't go fast but tackles the most difficult stony trails with aplomb.

Sunday 17 July 2005
We rose at 6.15 and were ready to leave at 7.30. The road up to the Castello reminded me of the dirt track in the Queyras we had done on the motorbike. Not surprising since we were less than 20 miles due south of where we'd been walking in 1995. The track ended in a wide grassy col and we geared up and started to walk in.

Scharlie slept rather badly, in spite of the comfort. She felt hot and her throat was bad. The campsite lights stayed on all night and helped her out when she emerged for a pee three times in the night! We have the convenience of a loo here, but her system won't oblige after all the travelling yesterday. However, we set off at 7:30 AM to climb the Roca Castello, one hour away above the campsite and dominating the skyline like the prow of a huge ship runing north-south. The rock is Triassic schistose quartzitet; steep but with plenty of holds.

Dimitri and teresa's yellow Kangoo

Roca Castello, east face, above Chiappera, Valle Maira

Last night there was a thunderstorm but today is cloudless and we climb easily through the alpine meadows. A herd of white cows has cleared the lower field of flowers but a little higher the land is rich in herbs and flowers, dominantly golden pink but touched with blue and white. Scharlie's head clears, her throat eases and she begins to feel better. Being able to recognise most of the species makes the climb to the col pass quickly.

At the head of the valley there is a monstrous concrete bunker with three staring eyes – blind now but built to man machine guns against the French. The border is very close here, Dimitri says. The bunker was never used because the Nazis beat the French in one day! I go inside, through a low tunnel to a central chamber. From this there are two smaller tunnels ending in a small concrete seat in front of the gun site. I can't help seeing a soldier sitting here in vigil, apprehensive.

We stop for a drink and a short rest. The mountain is huge above us and to me it looks impossible but I have learned that routes are quite different when you're on them and I have blanked out all anticipatory nerves. After further discussion and consultation of the oracle Dimitri and Mauri decide they know where our climb begins.

Finally, before we set off on the approach march, the guide to the cliff is

Scharlie looking out through gun embrasure in a concrete bunker

Scharlie begins the first pitch of 'Solo per Bruna' (5c 170m)

consulted. Now the mood is serious or, perhaps more accurately, anxious. Our chosen route is called *Solo per Bruna* and is grade 5. Unfortunately, the first pitches are hard. And as we walked over from Col Gregory, having left the sacks and put on our rock boots, we could see a line of bolts running up the grey wall. It looks steep and too hard but Dimitri says we won't know how hard it is unless we try, which is true of course. Climbs often look harder than they in fact prove to be and one's innate survival instincts kick in as one looks up at a steep wall from directly below.

We will climb in parties of three. The leader reaches the belay and the next two follow, almost together. It makes hard work for the leader and wearing helmets is obligatory.

Scharlie and I climb with Dimitri, and Teresa is on a rope with Mauricio and Walter. Dimitri climbs well but it doesn't look easy. Scharlie goes next and I followed 10 feet behind her. This is the way they climb here – two together; it means you have to trust the leaders rope work.

[Scharlie] I was glad the first pitch was hard as it gave me the opportunity to escape and wait at the bottom if I wanted to. I was also pleased that we would be returning to the same place so I could leave my sack – a good start. It went well and Dimitri, Steve and I soon reached a broad ledge two pitches up.

Mauri leading the following rope

Mauri climbing

[Steve] I found it hard and had to ask Scharlie how she had done one move where the handholds ran out. I figured you had to move left and she shouted that's right. We both got up quickly and the second pitch was much easier.

We now have a choice – to continue with a hard pitch or to opt to traverse to an easier route – called Gigismondo. We waited for the others. They took a long time, and were very slow. Teresa has not been climbing much lately, but in motherly style she carried a sack full of extra jackets, water and sweets. It felt like an hour before they appeared, so we decided to move to an easier route at this point, traversing to the north ridge, the *Cresta Sigismondi*, and following this to the summit. An easy pitch took as to the ridge, and suddenly we could look down a knife-edge, 400 metres vertically. It's impressive, says Dmitri you arrive in a protected way up a chimney and then … ooh!

[Scharlie] I allowed myself a single vertiginous glance and concentrated very hard on my hands and feet. This is only a grade pitch, says Dmitri. His rope work is good and over the years my technique of mind over matter has improved. It was exciting, pleasant and easy. The wind was fierce and I was extremely glad to have Teresa's jackets on the last belay. I rounded a spike and there was Dmitri smiling on the top with only 10 metres of flat ground between us. My world expanded again and I could stand and walk and look

Dimitri, Teresa, Walter and Mauri with Scharlie

Steve on summit with Provencale Cross, named after don Agostino Provencale, the parish priest who in 1850 made the first ascent to erect the cross.

around as if on the beach. On the summit there was a big ledge and we found a sheltered rock out of the wind in the sun and we went to sleep while we waited with equanimity for Mauri and Walter and Teresa with her *Fruta do Bocca* sweets.

[Scharlie] The abseil descent was equally exciting. Dimitri says it is completely safe. I know them well … it is only boring. He attached an extra prussic knot to the abseil rope, saying if you are unconscious the rope will lock – you don't need hands … perfect safety. I went over the edge with only a little shiver. A series of five vertical abseils which went well and then we were down safe, and in the sunshine. We took photographs of a gun emplacement from the war that was meant to defend Italy from the French. Back at the car we lounged around eating cheese, salami and beans then drove back to Campo Base for ice cream and coffee.

Rations tonight are relatively meagre – cheese biscuits and haricot beans in oil, but I don't feel hungry. We had to pitch the tent again, but last night's tent spot was taken so we find a new place nearer to the entrance. We fell asleep quickly and slept well until nearly 7, when we got up.

Scharlie abseiling off

Valle Gesso

Monday 18 July 2005

[Scharlie] I woke feeling ghastly again congested and sore throat turned to cough. The weather is bad and the decision is to drive to the Parco Argentère Naturel and walk to a refuge. The forecast says the weather will clear tomorrow. At the moment I have difficulty carrying myself and don't look forward to carrying a rucksack for two days. We set off about 8.30. Clouds gathered as we left. We are going to a valley parallel to the one we have been in, but further south. It is call Val di Gesso. Dimitri says this valley is very poor – it was the playground of the Kings of Italy in the 19th and early 20th century, kept to go hunting and to dally with the peasant women. The Royal family were from Savoy and they left Italy at the end of the war to save their own skins. They had remained uncommitted either to the fascists or the communists and the people had no respect for them, Dimitri says.

Scharlie slept most of the journey and woke when we stopped in Valdieri for

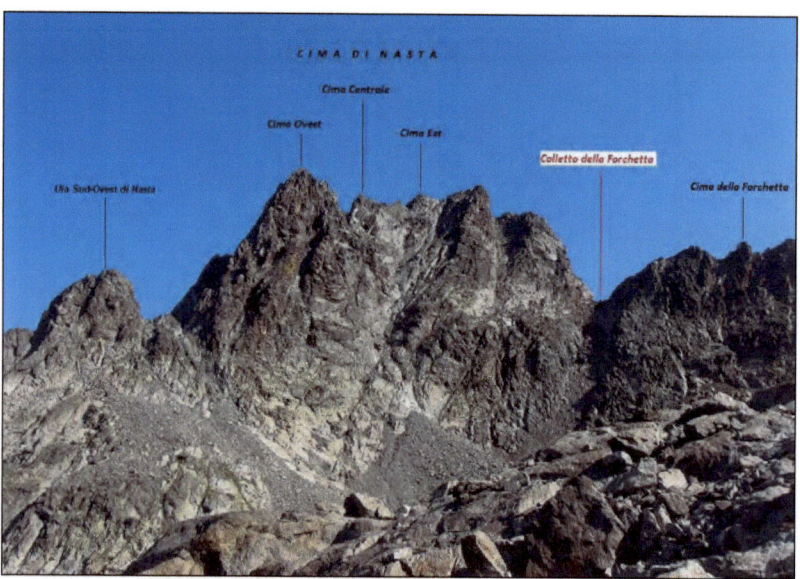

Cima do Nasta, Argentera massif, above Refuge Remendino

breakfast – coffee in the Bar Sport and panini, eaten in the park, the benches animated with old men enjoying the open air and women of the village – men at one end, women at the other. The thermal baths at the top of the valley are huge, but deserted. The road is unmade to the Refuge Regina Elena where our path begins. But this refuge is private and we are heading for the Refuge Remendino two hours climb away. At the head of the valley we drove past the barrier onto a stony track, which we followed to the end a mile or so further on. It was raining hard and a herd of the cows stood close together all pointing in the same direction. When the rain eased they broke rank and carried on chewing. I think they must disperse on the hill for some of the day and are then herded back into an area surrounded by an electric fence.

Dimitri has to go back down to the village to make a telephone call to a work colleague and Teresa stays with him while the rest of us start up the track to the refuge at 12.30. It starts to rain as we pack our sacks. We walk slowly, our heads down under our anorak hoods. We pass a big waterfall and finally reach the refuge below Cima Nastra. We have pasta and coffee and Steve Walter and Mauricio have a nap, leaving Scharlie writing postcards.

[Scharlie] To my surprise and relief the cool weather has revived my spirits and I am able to complete the steep two-hour walk without too much

Refuge Remendino 2430m, Argentera massif in background (Cima de Argentera 3287m)

difficulty. Most of the time the rain lashes and my trousers are wet against my legs but I enjoy the cool feeling. Steve is not so happy, he says he wishes he had his over trousers. I don't bring them because I feel bad wearing them when you haven't got any. Don't be, I reply.

We have some pasta for lunch with Mauri and Walter. The refuge is perched securely on a rock plateau below the snowline and the encircling peaks. Its bright red shutters look welcoming, even in the rain. Steve, Walter and Mauri go for a sleep but I read and write till Dimitri and Theresa arrive at 5pm. There

Steve seconding Dimitri on 'Relax' (4c, 10 pitches 450m) , Via Sud-Occidentale di Nasta

is a French group and an Italian family – grandfather, son and two boys but there's still plenty of room. We are all in room five and I choose a lower bunk for ease of getting out in the night. Lights out suddenly at 10 pm and once more I find myself unable to sleep. My cough and congestion has come back with a vengeance and now I'm coughing up stuff from my chest and sucking continuously on Olbas oil pastels to avoid disturbing the others. Steve has my earplugs and is fast asleep very quickly – once or twice I tried to turn him over because he's snoring gently. He jumps and stops. At midnight I creep out to the loo using the head torch and after that I sleep fitfully.

Tuesday 19 July 2005
[Scharlie] I'm feeling too ill to climb and when the others get up about seven, I stay put because I'm still feeling bad. Steve brings me café au lait in bed and that's great. The sky is cloudless blue again and they are going to climb so I decide to have my own rest day. The others pack their rucksacks and Mauri and Valter set off in front, climbing up through the boulder field and scree behind the refuge to patches of snow at the base of the cliff. I watch them hugging the cliff and becoming small moving points in no time at all. It's about

Steve on first pich of 'Relax.' First ascent: M. Benzi, B. Buffa and P. Cavallo 4 September 1994

Lago do Fremamorte, Valle Gesso, seen from high on Viva la Donna

9 am and I have a leisurely breakfast watching them. They are static at the bottom of the climb for a long time and I pack and order a sandwich and leave by 10.30. I have all day and no pressures to do anything but go at my own pace. I wonder how Chelo is and all the family at home but I keep my mind off work. I feel supremely relaxed and I'm so glad I came on this holiday.

[Steve] Our route, called *Relax* Grade 4c 450m, is just to the left of the waterfall that falls from the lake. I spot a bolt on the steep wall to the left of the easy rocks that Dimitri is exploring. Suddenly Mauri decides to take the lead. Dimitri is pleased; he says Mauri needs experience route finding. He also says Mauri is very self-conscious when climbing in front of a crowd.

Mauri goes slowly, trying to find his way. We are still in the shade and I have all my clothes on and am still freezing and I can't feel my toes. I put on my rock boots, thinking Dimitri and I should have gone first since we're faster and. Finally it is our turn to climb. The rock is much slippier than the quartzite of the Castello and I feel awkward with cold hands and feet. But I like the pitch and begin to trust the rock. It is gneiss and there are rounded footholds and incuts for the hands.

The second pitch is the hardest. It is a roof with two bolts for protection. The guide says it is athelitco. I'm still cold and off-balance and decide to pull on the rope sling that Dmitri has left for us. It is a mistake since it makes it even more strenuous. But I get up, feeling bad that I didn't use the rock.

There are seven more long pitches, some harder than others but generally about hard severe. The sun hits us and we warm up. But there is a cold breeze and I find I still need my fleece. I'm carrying a sack so could take it off as the sac will keep my back warm. But I try one pitch and I'm cold, so I put the fleece on again.

Mauri is quite slow at route finding and we don't reach the top until mid-afternoon. Teresa has brought food and we all sit on the top feeling good, looking at the view and savouring the rest before an abseil into the gully and a scramble down to the lake. Scharlie is there, sunbathing, and I shout down and ask her which way when I think we may have gone wrong.

We bathe our feet and start back to the hut. Again a good meal of pasta followed by stew; the blond guardienne is a great cook. As soon as we have finished eating I want to go to bed, but Scharlie persuades me to stay up a little

Steve nearing top of 'Viva le Donne' on Cima Paganini. (3051m)

longer until 9.30. The hut is much fuller than last night and there is a party of older Italians, all very fit looking, singing alpine choruses on the balcony as the sun sets behind a range of mountains to the north-west.

[Scharlie] I reach the bottom of the climb as they complete the first pitch and I am able to watch them all the way up. I walk a parallel line with their slab and ridge on my left. At the lake I stop and find a secluded shingle beach. The sun is bright but the air is cool, patches of snow that are still hard are melting into the clear water. I rest in the sun as they disappear from view, but I can hear cheerful shouts of voila and fantastique from Dimitri.

They are noisy climbers, quite unlike Steve's style, but Dimitri's enthusiasm is endearing and inspiring and Steve's strategy is to fit in; he doesn't actually join in the shouting though. The lake is a perfect place to watch the final ridge climb. It looks amazing and I wish I was up there but this is my sunbathing slot. I plaster on factor 30 cream balancing the desire to turn golden brown and reluctance to increase wrinkles.

At 4 pm they appear to have stopped for lunch on a flat bit below the top. Now they are abseiling down. *Libera, corda libera sono giù*, they call as they reach the end of the abseil and release the rope for the next person.

Teresa and Scharlie by Lago Fremamorte

Wednesday 20 July 2005

Dimitri knows the guardienne from a previous refuge. She is a good cook and last night we had a delicious soup followed by beef cut in very thin slices

Scharlie climbing 'Viva le Donne' (4c, D- 6 pitches 300m) on Cima Paganini. (3051m)

and cooked in wine and herbs. Scharlie is still feeling under the weather, but decides she wants to climb.

[Scharlie] This morning I'm feeling a little better in spite of more night coughing and we're off to climb *Viva Le Donne*, Hurray for Women, on Cima Paganini. It's about 40 minutes scramble over large boulders up to the snow line. Dimitri walks ahead of me with a slow precise rhythm. Climbing for him is all about preparation of the mind. Dreaming is for the mind, climbing is only for the body, he says. So he plans all the possible routes with great precision – this one he has copied out onto a piece of paper for easy access on the route. His tranquil swinging gait now is all part of the preparation and concentration

Our route is new and not in Dimitri's guidebook and I wonder if he will have remembered the route or made notes. The boulder field is complex and tiring. We reach a plateau and then climb a scree slope to the rocks. It is another slab and there are six pitches. Dimitri scrambles up to take a belay. We get into our climbing gear and Dimitri leads. I follow, then Steve. Mauri's group is second today. I find the first pitch easy but just hard enough to be interesting. The rock has great friction and sloping incut holes, which give me confidence. We climb fluidly and fast and the belay ledges are commodious. The second pitch is a little harder but the third is easy. I marvel at how much better I am feeling with height and I realise it is partly because I'm being looked after so well. Dimitri is

Scharlie on the penultimate hard pitch of Viva le Donne

superb with his rope work and I am climbing in the middle – all I have to do is unclip the runners. Steve does all the belaying, so I don't need to struggle with the way the rope is running or worry about whether I'm doing it right. If I'm going to get into climbing again I'll have to practice all this and get slick.

The first pitch is an easy warm-up and the second is steeper, but very enjoyable. The holes are smaller, but all are there. The next two pitches are easy then we reach a small stance below what looks like a huge overhang. I realise it is less than vertical but it looks much steeper. The previous stances have been big ledges we could sit on, now it is more serious.

The penultimate pitch is the hardest, ending in a small roof, which we climb on the left. It is a good line and exhilarating. Scharlie's feet shake on the small holds, but she's climbing well. I let her reach the second bolt before starting off after her. This is the way we climb, two together with Dimitri managing both ropes. The climbing is nice, quite technical, but there are good ledges every so often, where there are footholds, I can stop hands-free and take out the camera and get a shot of Scharlie climbing above me. I hope the photos give an impression of how dramatic it is. The final moves over the little roof at the top look sensational. When I get there I find good holds and get over elegantly. I am pleased with how well we have climbed. My instincts as so often

Scharlie on easy upper pitch of Viva le Donne

Lunch

now are to quit before I get started. But I managed to control my fear and say nothing and try not to think about the length of the route and how hard the final pitches might be.

Looking back at our route on Cima di Nasta

Scharlie abseiling

The next two pitches were VS English grade, not very hard at all, but it was delicate technical climbing on the spur – moving left and right to reach the holds. We belay on a large grassy ledge and scramble up the last easy pitch. It's not worth doing, so the others don't, and we return to the ledge for lunch. What a picnic site – bread, cheese, sausage and fantastic chocolate, coffee and sweets. Over 1,000 feet up!

[Scharlie] Then we began the long abseils. We had developed a rhythm of setting up the next abseil while the previous pitch was being cleared. Steve checks my abseil rope and we're off down in five abseils and I'm getting used to this.

We rested a short while at the bottom. Then we watched a walker ski down the snow in boots and no skis. It had looked flat from above, now we can see that it is quite steep. Dimitri tried on a lower slope, but not as successfully. We walked back to the refuge and repacked the sacks. The guadienne offers us a farewell Ginepe, homemade in the refuge from local juniper berries. We were all very convivial and we felt sad to be leaving. Dimitri with his Tuscan wit and cheerfulness is a favourite of hers.

Mauri is quiet and deeply bronzed with a wiry light frame and pixie ears. At first he seems to be glowering, then you see his eyes are just puckered against

Scharlie abseiling

the bright light. He is in love and rings his girlfriend every evening and returns to camp with a huge smile that transforms his face. He is kind, warm and observant and seems to anticipate things I need although he speaks no English. Silly me, he says pointing to his forehead. Not as bad as me I think. I've had more opportunity to learn. Walter is more withdrawn. He is keen on running and climbs well but without as much style as the others. He never leads and sometimes Dimitri is irritated by his caution and reluctance to try new routes but he has known him since they were at university together.

We walked down to the valley, catching final glimpses of the refuge, and our two routes. Dimitri wants to stay at a municipal campsite and go to Val di Gesso tomorrow. He's read about the superb ridge climb from a lake in a wild and beautiful place. It takes about three hours to walk there and we will bivi in the open air. I'm a little worried as my coughing is bad and my foot is giving me trouble after an hour's walk. The weather will decide, but discussion is all part of the process.

We drove back down Valle Gesso to Santa Anna a couple of kilometres above Valdieri, checked into the campsite and have another palaver. Mauri has disappeared to ring the girlfriend and we hang around for an hour because the showers are not open yet. Steve keeps saying he wants to eat and Dimitri

Descending from Argentere and Refuge Remendino

is hungry too but it's not clear what the plan is. Eventually Mauri returns and gives Steve a hug of apology. We set off back to the town he's just come from and park in the square where a band is tuning up. Once again we wait and chat but Steve and I don't know why. We wander up the street but the restaurant is closed, so we have to go all the way back to the campsite. It turns out that a refuge in Santa Ana has a restaurant but Dimitri thought it was closed for refurbishment. It's about 9 pm but we settle down to a huge meal. I have ravioli followed by Parma ham and melon and vitelli, a local delicacy of thinly sliced beef with mayonnaise sauce as starters. Then a Castell Magno gnocchi followed by more beef cooked in the local style in a wine sauce, again with lots of handmade breadsticks, fizzy young red wine and caramel cream to finish. We can hardly walk out of the building and collapse into bed. We felt stuffed. We had to put the tent up in the dark and I had a restless night, having eaten much too much. I coughed a lot but Steve has his earplugs so I don't need to worry.

We say goodbye to the Refuge Remendino wishing we could stay longer

Valle Orco

Thursday 21 July

As always things looked much better in the morning. But the forecast is not good – there is a depression centred on Britain – right on 56 Covent Garden, Dmitri says, which is affecting all the weather patterns in Italy. It will be unsettled till the weekend so the bivouac plan is out. We had a leisurely start getting out of the tent at 8.30. Dmitri has been up since seven and he and Teresa have been into Santa Ana for breakfast. Valter has been for a one-hour run. We use the excellent facilities on site and Steve pays for a lovely long hot shower together. Teresa mends a hole in her trousers, we have coffee and set off at about lunchtime, stopping to buy more cheese and post our postcards. We drive all day to reach Valle dell'Orco in the Gran Paradiso near Val d'Aosta. Valle dell'Orco means Valley of the Ogre.

We stop at the Albergo in the main square of Noasca. Dimitri and Teresa go for petrol and Mauri and Valter arrive. We go and look at the church and

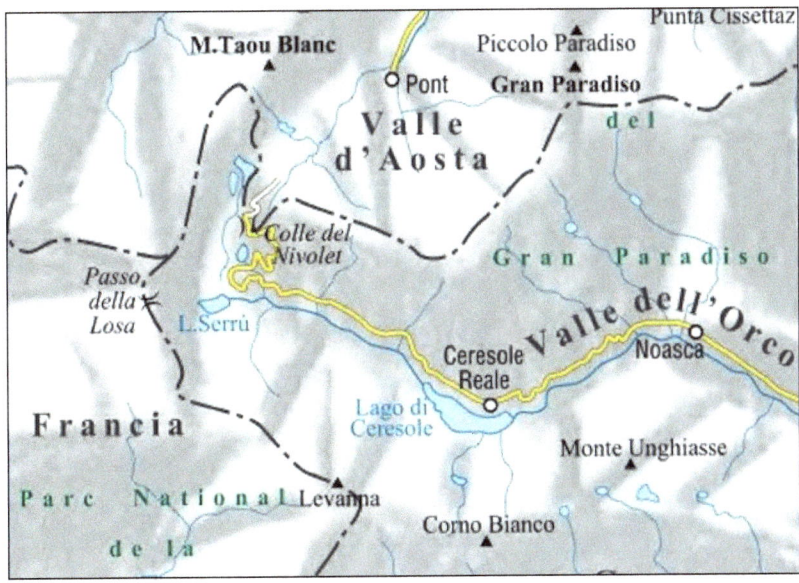

Valle dell'Orco, Gran Paradiso

after check out the hostel that they recommend.

[Scharlie] It's late when we get there and I'm feeling terrible. My stomach is bloated and I feel headachy and congested. I'm feeling too sick to walk to the waterfall nearby or take in the geological display in the tourist centre. I think I look bad and Mauri is insistent that we should consider staying in a hostel instead of camping. He stayed there before and with great alacrity accompanies us to help interpret. I mime that we just want to investigate and this turns out to be almost an Italian word. He understands and asks the proprietress to show us the *camera matrimoniale*. It looks heavenly – the great white bed and ensuite bathroom; I had been expecting more bunks. My thoughts turned to the possibility of amor even though I'm still feeling so ill. The lady says she'll keep the double bed for half an hour, after that will have to have one with twin beds.

We meet Dimitri and Teresa in the cafe to discuss the plan but after another glance at my face, Steve says he'll go back and book. The room is nice so Steve booked two nights. They all seem to think this is the best thing for us, to stay in the hotel, as Scharlie is still unwell. The others will be camping free by a river, where they had been before. There is grass and larch trees and huge rounded granite boulders and a slate table, everything you need, Dimitri says, with an

Noasca, Valle Orco, Parco Nazionale Gran Paradiso

expansive gesture.

The forecast is poor for tomorrow and for the weekend but we'll have to see. The hostel is nice; the room has a double and single bed a large bathroom. The only problem is that they don't start serving breakfast till 8.30 and Dimitri is coming to pick us up an hour earlier at 7.30.

[Scharlie] Teresa has a great feast ready – anchovies in basil and oil and chunky bread, tomato salad, pasta and Parmesan. I relax and feel much better. After supper I wander along the river looking for pebbles. Mauri and Walter want to take us to a lake, Bella Bella, they say, further up the valley so we race along in convoy first up a twisty disintegrating road through the woods and suddenly emerge into a wide modern tunnel through a gallery window. Often these experiences feel surreal because we never know what's going to happen. I understand very little of the constant flow of Italian and Steve, who does much better, sometimes picks up the wrong end of the stick.

There is a small bar near the lake and I make the mistake of accepting the offer of a drink from Mauri and ordering ginepe. She gives me a huge glass and I have a sip or two then decant most of it into an empty plastic bottle. It'll last the rest of the holiday! We are well ready for bed and grateful when they drive us back to the hostel. I'm able to pile up the pillow so I'll cough less.

Lago di Teleccio, Vallone di Valsoera, Valle Orco, Parco Nazionale Gran Paradiso

Friday 22 July 2005

[Scharlie] I wake at six and doze for half an hour before getting up and having a shower so we'll be ready when Dimitri arrives. Dimitri is collecting us at 7.30 am so they've laid out breakfast for us in the TV room. There are two large thermoses of hot milk and water but they prove to be tepid. They are only token thermoses, says Steve. I pack up the bread and marmalade and we join the others. We go for a coffee in the bar in the square before heading off down the valley.

I'm not climbing today as I'm quite weak and puffy eyed. Mauri really wants Steve to do *Pesce d'Aprile* with him and is all smiles and inducements. I can see Steve is feeling torn but his trepidation wins. I want to stay with Dimitri and be looked after, he says. I know the feeling so well. Mauri and Walter stay near the campsite, while we drive for 40 minutes to a dam – the water supply for Turin. The road leads up a wild valley, the only sign of habitation tumbledown old buildings with stone roofs and cows lifting their heads as we pass. I don't understand why this is not developed, says Steve. Dimitri says it's further from the main road for climbers and not economic for locals to farm. But the real reason is one we know well. It is in the national park and difficult to get permission to build.

Noastca

[Steve] Mauri and Valter are going to climb *Pesce d'Aprile* just over the road and want me to go with them, but I have decided to go with Dimitri. I fancy going up higher and don't feel like being frightened on a route that Teresa says she found very hard. Maybe I have made the wrong decision. Mauri is very disappointed, but this way Scharlie and I stay together and she gets to do a nice walk rather than hang around the village.

We drive to Rosone and then turn off the main road onto an access road built for the dam at the head of the valley. We drive up the precipitous switchback road past notices saying Private Road, Danger, No Admittance until we reach a parking area next to the dam. From here we walk an hour to the Refuge Pontese above the Lac di Telessio with its almost unreal glossy green water.

[Scharlie] The road starts to rise in a tight series of bends. From below, the wall they are about to climb seems almost vertical. It reminds me of the road to Newcastle when we near the top, with massive concrete buttresses to stick the road to the cliff. We park at the top under huge ugly buildings, which seem obsolete now. Maybe there were for building the dam. The dam itself is pleasant and curving, holding back the blue green melt water. Dimitri hasn't been here before, but we're walking up to the refuge where Walter says there

Valle dell'Orco

are some short climbs on the slabs. I'm not climbing but I want the exercise. I'm fascinated by the flora, in some ways so similar to Leveret Croft. The soil looks a bit like shale, and chives, thymes, birds foot trefoil and devils bit scabious flourish with great profusion and variety. I think that I might be able to encourage more things like this in Bills Field and pocket a soil sample.

The roof of the Refuge Pontese is painted bright yellow with matching shutters and is a welcoming sight against the jagged amphitheatre high mountains. A fast tumbling stream flashes past us on its way to a gash in the cliff face and then cascades down to the lake. A group of friendly milk-smelling cows make music as they enjoy the rich herbs of the meadow. Only the females have bells – maybe the size of the bell goes with seniority. Steve says if you're a cow it's better to be born a girl, as a frisky and carefree young bullock eyes us inquisitively.

The Guardienne, a brunette this time, is as equally delightful as the blonde at the last refuge. She has lively eyes and a climber's physique. Scharlie reckons she must be a climber. But it turns out that she isn't. She has two children – a boy of about six and a girl of nine or 10. They are here for 4 to 6 months, so maybe they go to school in the village or she teaches them herself. We have coffee and apricot juice and Teresa suggests a slice of scrumptious homemade roof and apple cake. I buy a slice to take with me and Steve says he hopes there will be some left when he gets back.

[Steve] We get geared up for climbing. Our chosen route is *Via Cochise* in the Vallone di Piantonetto. It is a long series of holdless slabs at an easy angle bit with little for the hands and occasional bolts for protection. It is only a short way away, so we put on our climbing harness and follow the main path up the

Refuge Pontese and Lago di Teleccio,

mountain for a short while and cross a bridge over the river. There is a herd of chamois that depart efficiently as we approach and a herd of cows with their many jangling bells.

We climb a small knoll overlooking the slabs we have come to climb and find a belay from which we can abseil. We do five abseils down the slabs, which look exceedingly devoid of holds. Scharlie is perched on a slab to our right looking out. The slab is convex and steepens below her. If she slips she will fall 1,000 feet. It gives me the ebbie geebers and I ask her to find a place higher up on the path. We descend out of her sight and she decides to go for a walk.

The first pitch has a very hard move and we all end up pulling on the bolt. The middle three pitches are slightly easier. It is tiring as there is hardly anything for the hands. But once you realise that your feet will stick if you find the slightly better places, where there is a depression or extrusion on the blank face, you just trust your feet and pad up the bare rock. The final pitch is hard but I manage it all right, having got into a rhythm.

[Scharlie] We walk a short distance from the refuge to the top of the cliffs where Steve Dimitri and Teresa will abseil down to climb the slabs. I tried to find a good place to photograph them but Steve gets very jumpy. I can't see that I'm sitting unroped at the top of a large smooth slab that slopes endlessly

Refuge Pontese with its bright yellow roof and shutters

'Via Cochise' (5c 200m) slab with no handholds and little for the feet

'Via Cochise'

"down to the lake. You'll only be able to see us if you follow the path up, Steve shouts. I take his advice and look for the red waymarks. I'd intended to spend the time writing and sunbathing, but the path is beguiling and before I know it I am high on the mountain near waterfalls. I'm going away from the lake so after a while I contour round towards the slabs but find I still can't see them.

I squeal as a large grey bird erupts from under my feet and runs with its wings trailing to hide under a rock. It must be some sort of grouse. I sit in the sun and eat my bread and cheese and apple cake. There's not a single person in that huge area of meadow and mountains and I feel happy. I hear Steve shout and can see them emerging from the depths on the last two pitches. It has been hard work – you have to trust your feet and just keep going. There's nothing for the hands. Steve wonders whether he should have gone with Mauri but he'd have missed this refuge which is magnificent in its setting. Dimitri says if you can make another week to come back we will stay here and plan everything. There are some long ridge routes, which look good. In the hut we have more coffee and cake and managed to get in first this time and pay and we buy a T-shirt made in Mexico with a smiling sun face as a birthday present for Jessica.

We walk back to the refuge and when we get there the guardienne is

Teresa following on 'Via Cochise'

cooking supper and we order coffee and cake. The homemade apple cake is moist and superb. Finally, and a little regretfully, we head off down to the valley. If we hadn't booked the hotel, Dimitri would have liked us to stay here the night and climbed higher tomorrow. This is not to be and we say we'll come back next year.

On the way back we stop so Scharlie can examine a flat roof, rather like the barn roof at Leveret Croft, but here the roof has a froth of sedum flowering on top – more inspiration for home. We may try and do something similar. Later, after a meal by the river of anchovies and parsley followed by pasta and a tuna salad, we go back up the valley to the refuge Massimo Mila in Caracole. One wall of the refuge has holds bolted on it to make a climbing wall and I suggest we might do the same for the children on the end wall of the barn at Leveret Croft. Then it's back to the hostel.

[Scharlie] Teresa cooks a mix of fried chilli beans, tuna and oil for dinner, eaten outside by the river. It tastes great. The first time today I am feeling well with a bubble of energy inside me. I fancy going for a walk with Steve to the cascade in the village, then a shower and bed but we find us in the back of the car on the way through the tunnel to the lakeside bar. This time I only order hot chocolate with cream and its thick and delicious. The bar is in a refuge named after an Italian music theorist who was imprisoned for being an antifascist but survived to become a prolific climber and lover of nature.

[Steve] Scharlie can't find her bag with book and journal and instead of helping her properly I suggest she had too many bags to keep track of. So we get to bed at odds, which is sad, but we have a look and in the morning and it turns up in Dimitri's van.

[Scharlie] We are tired by the time they drive us back and I get out of the car with an armload of belongings because I haven't got my big sack with me. In the room I realise my little plastic bag with my most personal belongings is missing – book, journal, pen, glasses, purse. I can't remember what I did with it when I got in the car and I'm afraid it's fallen out of my sack. We ring Dimitri but he doesn't answer. Suddenly everything becomes bleak and impossible. My inability to keep track of my belongings is a never-ending trial. My throat feels scratchy and my eyes are bleary. We both feel as if the evening is ruined. There is no hot water so we can't have a shower. Steve says you lost it because you had too many things all over the place. This remark interferes with my painful reconstruction of what I did with the bag. You can't take criticism, he says. Neither can you, I reply. But you do criticise me, he says. We are on a rollercoaster ride to nowhere good. We shut up and get into bed and I feel rigid with unhappiness. How can such a little thing turn everything upside down? I wonder. Steve hugs me and says he's sorry he is not more encouraging.

'Legolas Tutti Libre', Piramide, Valle dell'Orco

Constant alarms about losing things get me down sometimes, he says. I say that I think he's very patient considering. We leave a message on Teresa's answerphone to check the car and the campsite. I have one long coughing fit about 3 am but otherwise I sleep deeply.

Saturday 23 July 2005
Steve wakes me from a deep sleep and I look at my watch – it's 6.30 am and Dimitri says he's not collecting us till 8.00 so I wish Steve had left me longer but I don't fuss because we have to pack everything to vacate the room and I want to shower. I stagger into the bathroom and feel revived and rewarded for my prompt response as I enjoy the shower. Steve is all ready but I don't rush as I packed most of my stuff last night. As I'm cleaning my teeth Steve says, shall I go down? Don't rush yourself – you have time. I wonder why he's in a hurry. If you go down won't it provoke him into getting breakfast too early, I say? I'm looking at my watch and thinking it's only 7 am. I don't want more coffee. Steve grunts and suddenly I realise it's actually 8. In my befuddled state I'd forgotten to add on the Italian extra hour. I bundle my last things into my sac and rush downstairs where Steve is waiting to put things in the car.

Teresa says there's more bad news – Dimitri has gone to buy the papers. You have your breakfast here and we'll meet you in the cafe. It turns out that a young Brazilian man has been shot by mistake by police outside Stockwell underground station. It appears to have been the worst form of uninformed panic reaction by the security officer. I feel very angry and remember how threatened and confused I myself have felt when confronted by armed men in a country were I am a tourist.

We drive up the valley to near the Kosterlitz crack, the test piece none of us could get off the ground on the other evening. We plan to climb Nautilus on Sergeant Crack, but for some reason, maybe it looks too hard, we jumped back in the vehicles and head back to the campsite.

We arrive and gear up immediately. This time Scharlie comes and Teresa says. Dimitri explains we are going up to climb *Legolas Tutti Libre*, a line that starts off left of the Pierre Allain Fissure on the Pyramide and finishes right. Again the first pitch is hard, but we climb it well. Then Scharlie has difficulty with a high step on pitch three and I have to give her a boost. There are four pitches in all, and the climbing is more varied than yesterday. The last pitch is 5C and in a roof. Valter makes it look quite hard, so Dimitri takes a line to the left of the roof it is very pleasant.

[Scharlie] We're climbing in the valley by the campsite today. It's my last chance and I'm feeling a lot better. Dimitri chooses a climb nearby. Teresa is

Legolas Tutti Libre', Piramide, Valle dell'Orco

'staying with the campsite today. We clamber a short distance over boulders in birch woodland to the base of the cliff. This is granite and much smoother than my other climbs. Another route called *Fissure Pierre Allain* follows a crack line, which slants reassuringly near our line. There's a difficult move to get onto the slab and not a great deal in the way of holds but I do it reasonably well. I'm glad the first pitch is the hardest. I joined Dimitri on the ledge feeling pleased. You did well, he says. The second pitch is supposed to be easier but I have

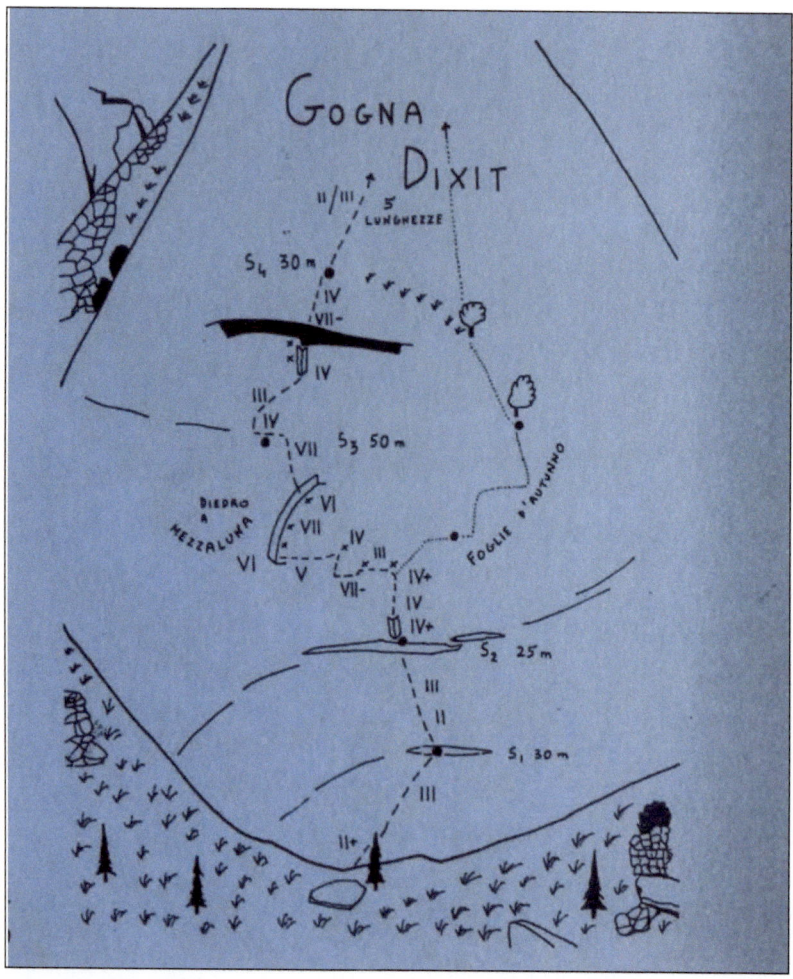

Cavalieri perdenti 'Gogna Dixit' (5b 300m) Alessandro Gogna, Gabriele Beauchod, Marco Marantonio on 12 July 1980. First climbed free by Bruno Baima in the middle of the 90s

a huge struggle getting started. In the end I get fed up and Steve gives me a leg up. It's not easy to reach the holds and there are no firm places to pause. I have to squirm around a small birch tree before moving up again. When we watched Dimitri doing it Steve called out, poor tree. Dimitri thought he said 4D and called out no grade 3. We all agreed on the ledge that this was under graded. Mauri and Walter were well ahead of us and we could see then heading for the final pitch, which pulled over a roof that was billed as 5, but could be avoided. We decided to avoid it and Dimitri move diagonally across to the left to do the Pierre Allain finish.

I have adjusted to the smooth rock and climb quite well until I reach the last moves on the wall just below Dimitri. I had to reach out in a bridging position to my right toe just reached a hold but I found I couldn't step up on my left leg to reach a secure hold a long way up. I didn't really feel scared, just weak. I kept saying I can't push up and when Dimitri reached out I grasped his hand with alacrity. I felt a bit cross with myself for not having tried – if I fallen off he would easily have held me, but all things considered it was good climb.

As usual we rappel down the route. We have a coffee and then Dimitri is raring to go again. This time the chosen route is harder at 5C. He says it is very famous because of the team that climbed it and because it was a climb

Slabs of Gogna Dixit'

of advanced difficulty in the 80s. It is called. *Cavalieri Perdenti*, also known as *Gogna Dixit* after the first climbed ascentionist. There are four pitches again and a much longer walk up through thorn scrub. It is harder than the first route and more technically varied. We begin to enjoy ourselves and find we are climbing well.

The second pitch is reputedly the hardest, but we find them all about the same standard. This there are couple of hard moves on the first pitch and then a small belay before the overlap pitch. The overlap is like a crescent moon. There is a small indefinite crack that one can lay back on and I work my way up to the very top of the Crescent and get a good right-hand hold before stepping over onto the slap to the left. The third pitch is also holdless, but we are over halfway and we feel good.

We made it down in two abseils with Mauri leading – the first one was very long and scary to start as it went right over the roof. We have bread and cheese followed by wild cherries from the tree next to the first belay and wild raspberries on bushes all the way down to the road.

When we get back we find a group of men stocking the river with trout. We sit by the river and have coffee and a rest. We are watching a group of men who were emptying farming buckets into the water. We go near and see dozens of fish lying on their backs with their gills pulsating in distress. There is going to be a fishing competition later today and they have brought trout from a fish farm. The journey took longer than expected, it was very hot today, and many of the fish are expiring. When put into the river they were stunned by the cold water. We joined the men in gently turning the fish over and cradling them until they started to swim. Some of them regained control and started to move within the water currents. Some of them, especially the large ones, turned onto their backs again and died. Watching them I realise that fish, like birds, have to learn to deal with the power of the elements they live in. These fish brought up in a tank were experiencing for the first time the speeding chaos of fast water flowing over and around rocks. Under our fingers their small bodies felt soft and delicate. We enjoy helping revive them by turning them over and helping kick-start them back to life. We watch one caught in an eddy and thrown into a frothing channel as it plunged between two rocks.

The men seemed a little upset by the numbers of dead fish. Those that are not dead now will be dead by this evening the organiser lugubriously told us. The competition starts with a bang of a firework at 2 o'clock and fish are caught furiously for the first 10 minutes or so. Then it settles down with only the four or five experienced fishermen catching any. They are fishing with collapsible rods and spinning reels and using a variety of live bait. Some of them are better than others. Three of them are particularly fascinating – a grey bearded bloke on the opposite bank, who is very energetic, a grey-haired man on our side who seems very wily and fishes the shallow pools with tiddlers before tackling the faster water and the organiser in a yellow T-shirt who pops his catch into a plastic bag tucked into the back pocket of his waistcoat.

The fishing competition finishes at 6 and we wonder who won. They're setting up a tarpaulin and tables and obviously plan to cook and eat the catch. I imagine they caught practically all the fish that survived the release. Scharlie hopes that they enjoyed the three hours of freedom. Mauri and Teresa went off to the shop for the evening meal while Walter, Steve and Dimitri decide to do one last climb while Scharlie stays by the river.

We had thought that we would be staying here the night but there is obviously going to be a rowdy party. When they get back quite suddenly Dimitri gets up and suggests we leave. So we pack the van and say goodbye to Mauri and Valter who are going to climb near Bologna and drive through the evening and get back to Florence at 1.30.

We pack the van and say goodbye to Valle dell'Orco

Sunday 24 July 2005

We sleep until 10 or 11 and, after a shower, have a late lunch. We stay at the table chatting about the future. We are pessimistic that there doesn't seem an attractive alternative to market capitalism. Theresa is tired but is patient and finally we go off for a siesta about five. They ask us what we'd like to do when we wake and Scharlie says she'd like to go out to eat. We go to a place that Dimitri's father likes. The tables are in the open under pine trees that form the roof. We get to bed late again.

We are up early at seven and Dimitri and Teresa run us to the airport. They have been so kind and generous to us the whole holiday.

Lago di Teleccio,, Valle dell'Orco

Valle Garrafano, Apuane

Thursday 21 July 2004

We arrive in Pisa by ferry from Coirsica and say farewell to Axel and Gabi and the boys who we have been walking the GR20 with and are whisked away in Dimitri's yellow Kangoo, straight to the Apuane.

After a couple of hours drive we reach Carolino's restaurant in the mountains. The proprietor, Paolo, is the spitting image of Robert de Niro. Later we learn that Paolo's father spent twelve years in America, so maybe they're half-brothers!

The place, Dimitri says, is very special. The food, cooked by Paolo's wife, Sandra, is superb. We have a huge antipasto, followed by trout and crème caramel. With unlimited wine, the bill comes to 23 Euros each. Sandra doesn't live here. She lives with her mother in her own house and he lives here with his mother.

Dimitri has been talking about where we would spend the night. It sounds like a refuge. He shrugged when we ask. It turns out to be a lean-to that he

Apuane

and his climbing friends helped Paolo convert into a bunk-house. It has ten beds, a stove, a hot water shower and toilet. Electricity is provided by a water wheel.

Sunday 5 June

We sleep well and wake just before seven. We expect breakfast but Dimitri is worried about the weather and wants a quick getaway. We drive through the sunlit Garrafano valley and stop in Castel Nuovo, where Theresa said they had been married, We meet the others in the tiny square and have coffee and croissants in the restaurant. The team obviously always meet here to reunite before driving to the crags.

We climb a quarry road until we reach a parking place next to the old refuge they are remodelling as a hotel. We pack the rucksacks with the two ropes and climbing gear Dimitri is lending us. We climb up through the quarry. It's amazing. They have been taking marble from here for ever. The block for Michelangelo's Pieta came from here. Dimitri says one of the mountains is so honey-combed with caves you can use your mobile phone deep underground.

From the quarry we climb a forest trail to a col. From here we have two

Marble quarry Castel Niovo, Valle Garrafano , Apuane

choices – the Diedro Sur at 4c or a long ridge of 3c. We choose the ridge. Dimitri has done it twenty times at least. But he's worried that it will rain and there are lots of places to escape from it back down to the road.

Last night he'd been talking about a route of 5c called Banda Bailar. We wonder if we can still climb 5c. We needn't have worried – the plans have changed and ambitions reduced in the light of morning and we are going to do a grade 3 ridge. We gear up and Dimitri leads off with Guiseppi. Scharlie and I follow on a separate rope. Behind us there are three other ropes – Mauricio, who we climbed with in Como, and Laura who I climbed with in Chamonix. Behind them Franco and Walter, who were also in Chamonix. And behind them, two young guys, Paolo and Jacobo. Dimitri is a veritable pied piper.

The first couple of pitches are nice – quite steep but with lots of holds. The grade is about HVD, but the problem is the rock is loose and you have to test every hold. We climb steadily towards the first tower, then abseil down and walk to a col.

Dimitri knocks down a big block. There is a rattle of stones, then a strangled scream. A party are struggling up the path to the col from Vinci, a small village in the valley. One of the walkers yells and gesticulates at Dimitri, who is totally unmoved and shouts back. When we meet up with them their tempers

Steve begins climbing the ridge

seemed to have recovered and all seems forgotten.

There are four more pitches to the final summit. Scharlie changes into her boots. The final pitch is quite hard but she manages it fine. We have been climbing together, the three leading ropes inter-twined. The other three parties have disappeared. They had been trailing a long way back and Dimitri says they decided to descend from the col. My left knee feels weak and it has been hard to step up on some of the holds. Now we coil the ropes and pack the gear. I change into my boots and we begin the long descent. It's steep slabs

Steve begins climbing the ridge

interspersed with scree, broken ground and patches of snow.

My knee aches and it seems never-ending. Scharlie bounds head, delighted for once to leave me struggling. But when we finally reach the quarry road Dimitri says it's only been fifteen minutes. I can't quite believe it and look back at the summit in amazement. We are both tired but the light is beautiful. It's about six o'clock and the weather has been perfect all day – cool and sunny.

We meet up with Mauricio and Laura and drive back through the Garafano in the evening sun and get back to Carolino's as it's getting dark. We pack while Dimitri is having coffee. Paolo and Sandra are in expansive mood and farewells take a while. Dimitri says he had been coming here for ten years before Paolo exchanged more than two words. with him. We get back after midnight and go straight to bed.

Monday 7 June, Pisa
We wake about eight when Dimitri's phone goes. It's his boss, Cerrutti, who always starts work early and likes to torture his subordinates. He'd promised to ring this afternoon, but said he'd forgotten. Theresa goes to work after breakfast and we repack, putting all the heavier stuff in the hand luggage to

Scharlie leading on the ridge

avoid having to pay excess baggage. We drive to Pisa and park as near as we can to the old centre.

We walk to the Leaning Tower. Dimitri says the Piazza around the cathedral is the best bit of Pisa. The stonework has just been cleaned and gleams white against the bright green lawn. There are lots of Chinese tourists. They all want to have their photo taken holding up the tower.

Dimitri says he did his PhD here and had to come two or three times a week by train. Pisa is a university town like Cambridge, but the main subjects

Nearing the summit

Scharlie and Dimitri on the belay

The summit

here are literature and humanities so there isn't the spin-off industry. He finds the café he used to frequent and we have a snack before he runs us to the airport. Italian airports are so much more relaxed than English ones. We have a last coffee and catch the plane home

Scharlie in Pisa

www.ingramcontent.com/pod-product-compliance
Lightning Source LLC
Chambersburg PA
CBHW042338150426
43195CB00001B/37